This book belongs to

_____

Copyright 2020
Author and illustrator: Laurette Seddon
Instagram: @lolla_doesstuff

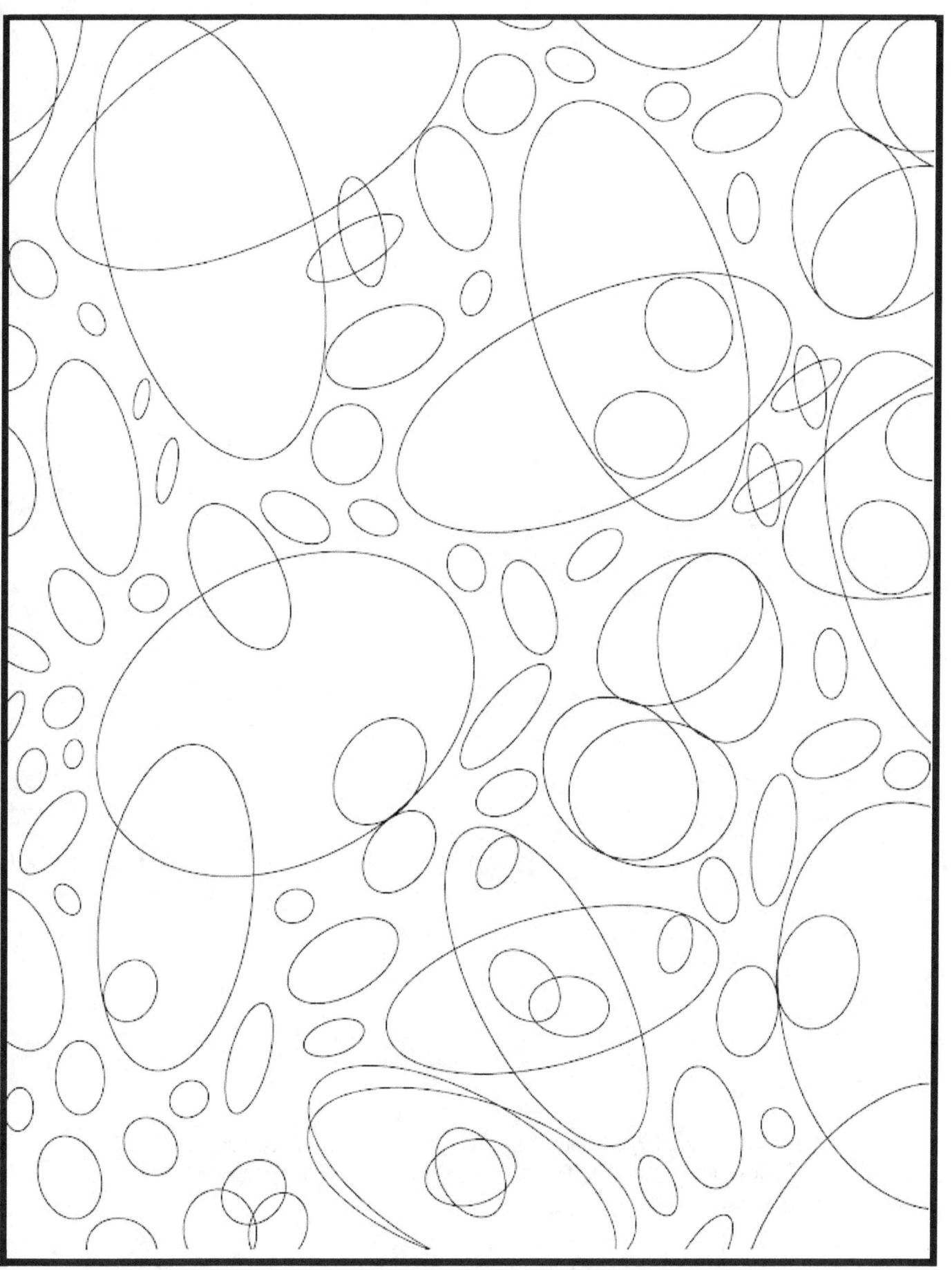

Colouring challenge: try using only contrasting colours
Contrasting examples: Blue & Orange, Red & Green, Yellow & Purple

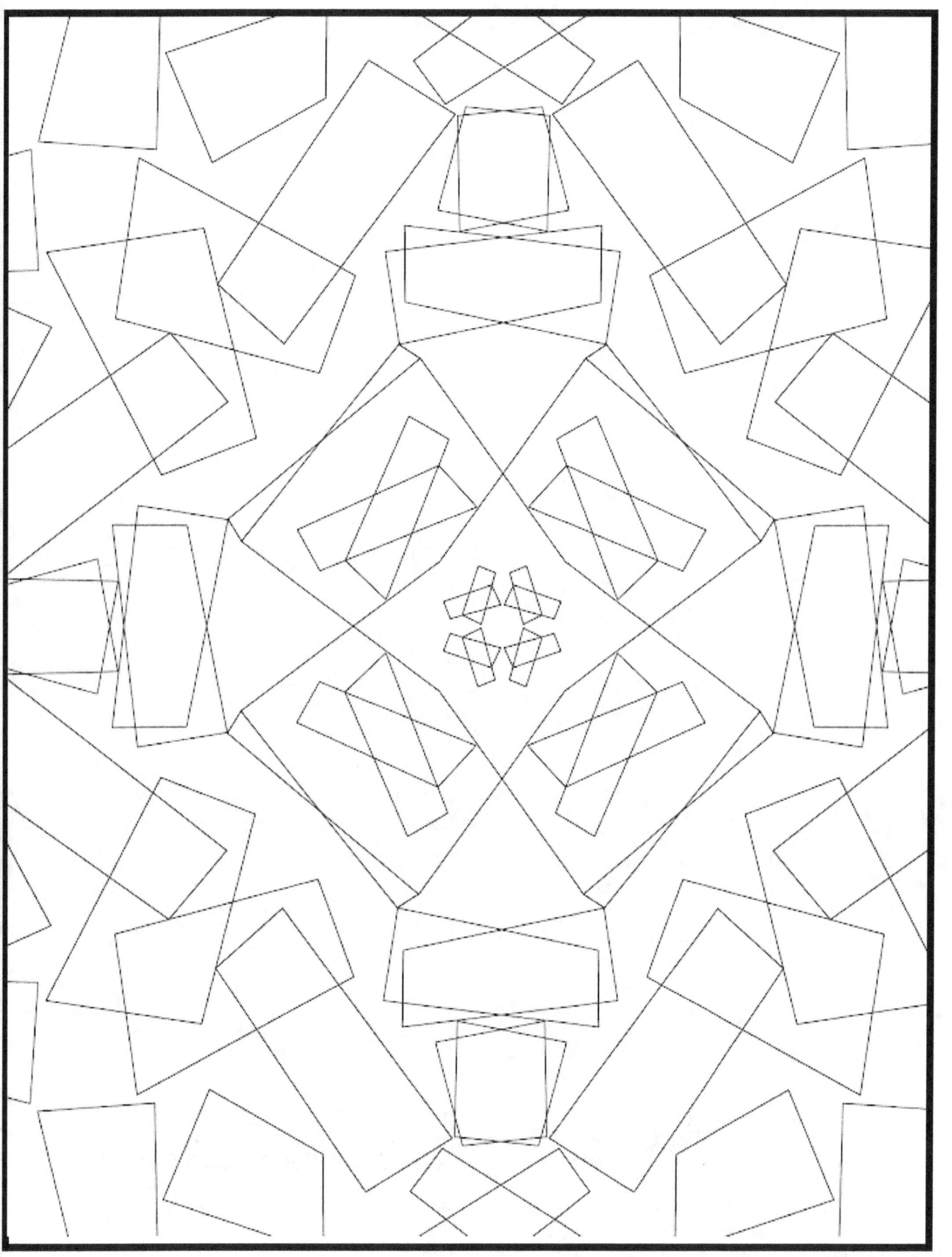

Colouring challenge: try using only complimentary colours
Complimentary examples: Yellow & Green, Blue & Red, Yellow & Red

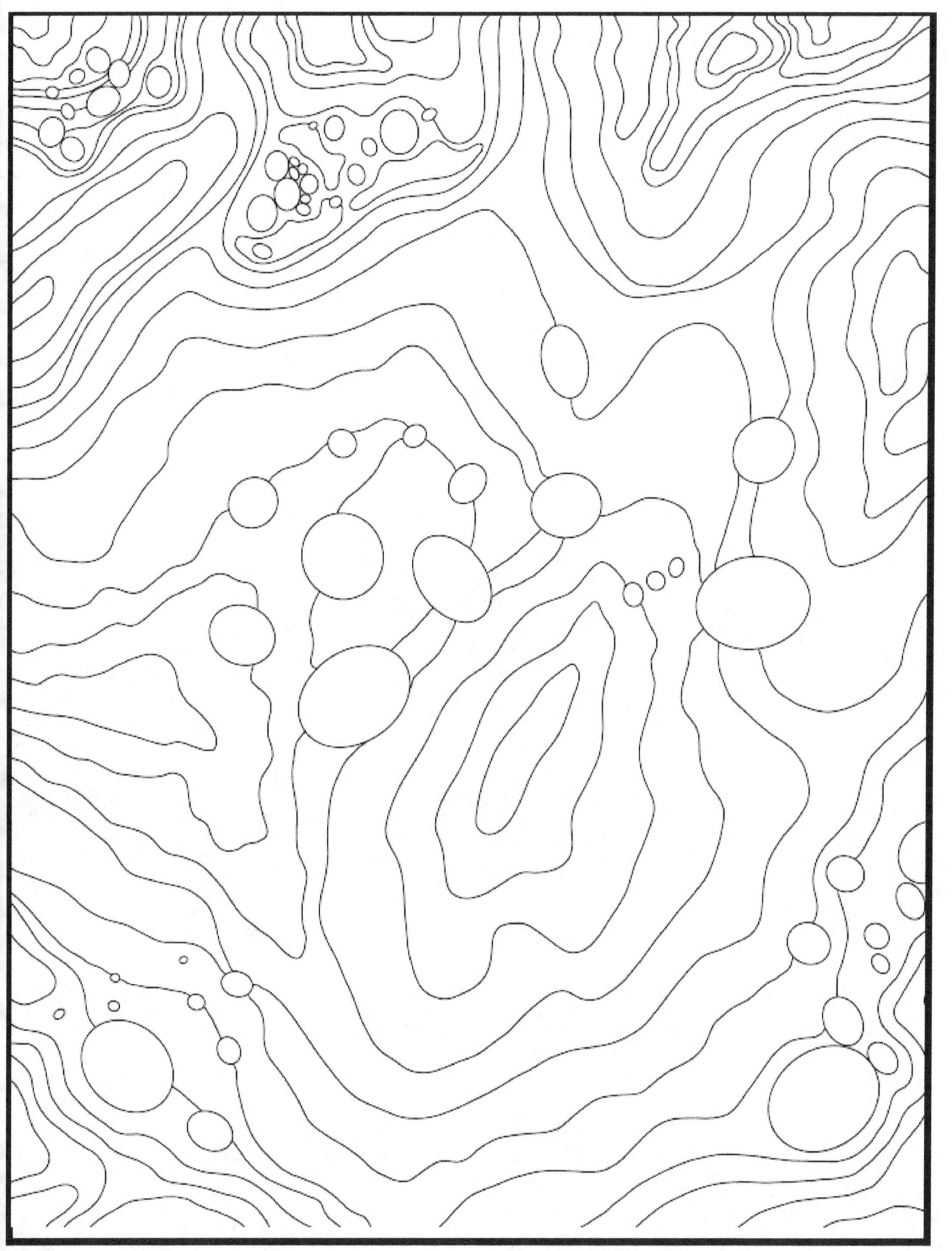

Colouring challenge: try using only hues of one colour
Hue examples: Yellow orange, Yellow, Green yellow

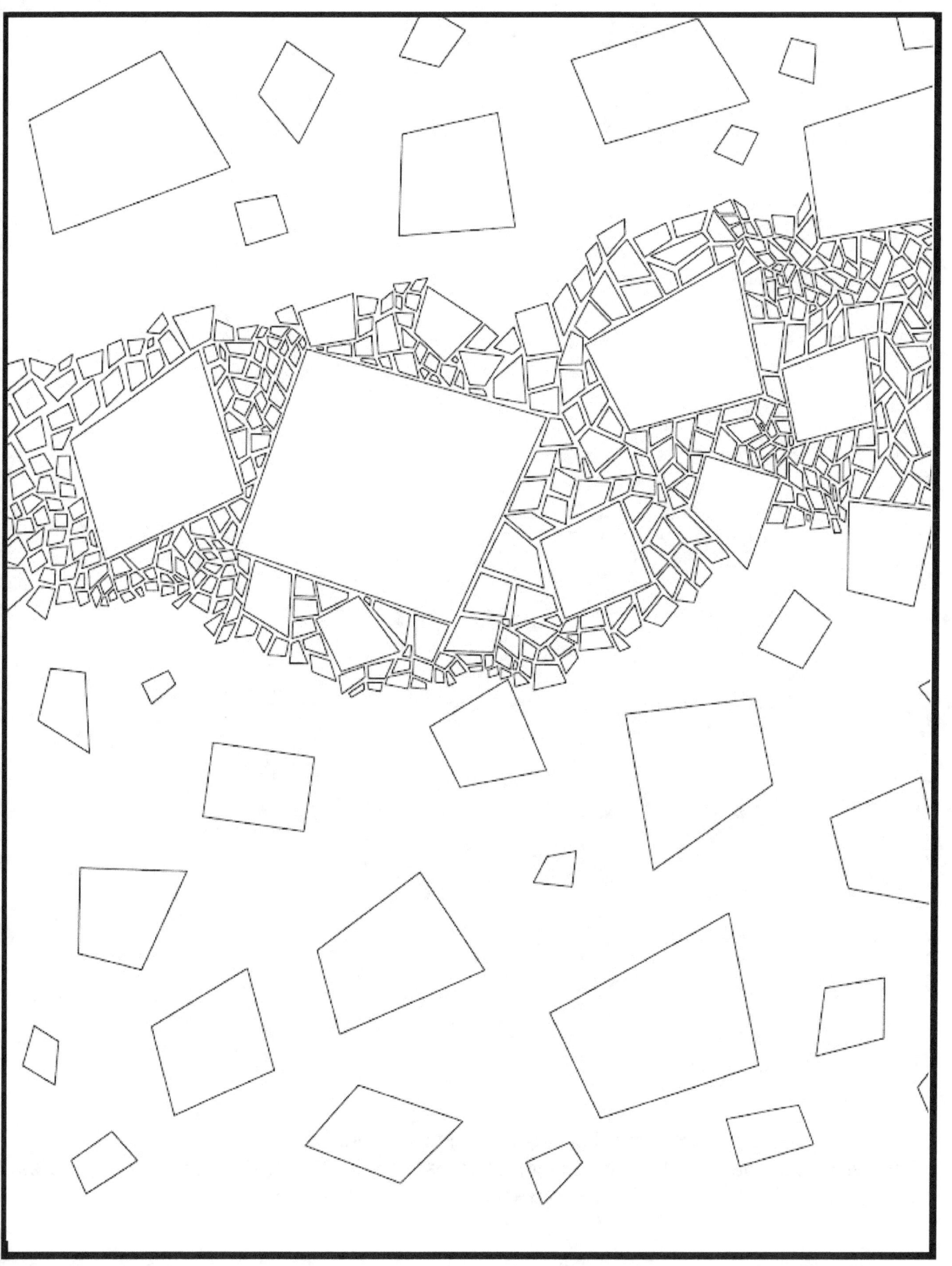

Colouring challenge: try using four random colours
Randomising methods: have a family member choose, blindfold yourself, pour out your supplies and choose those pointing North

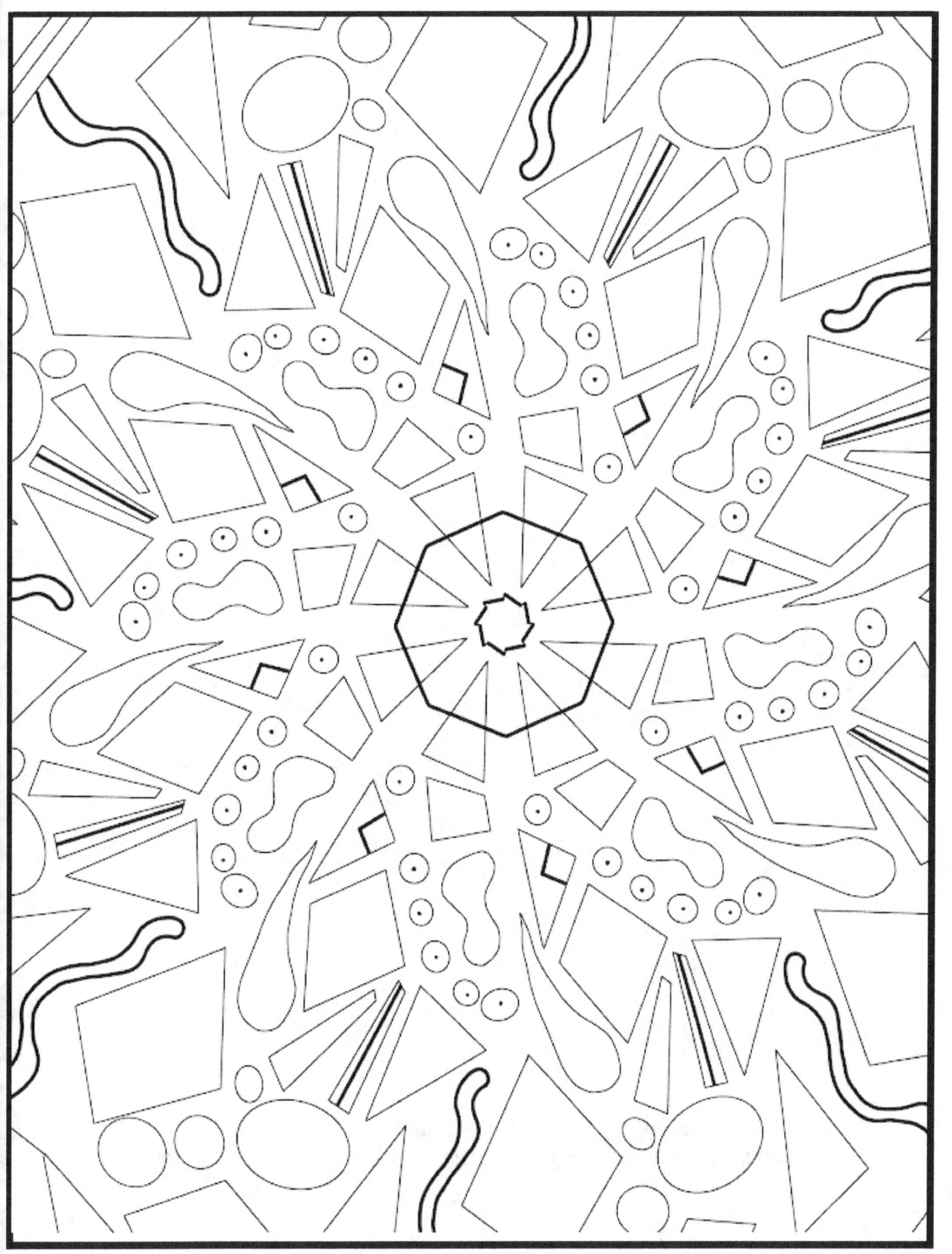

Colouring challenge: try using only contrasting colours
Contrasting examples: Blue & Orange, Red & Green, Yellow & Purple

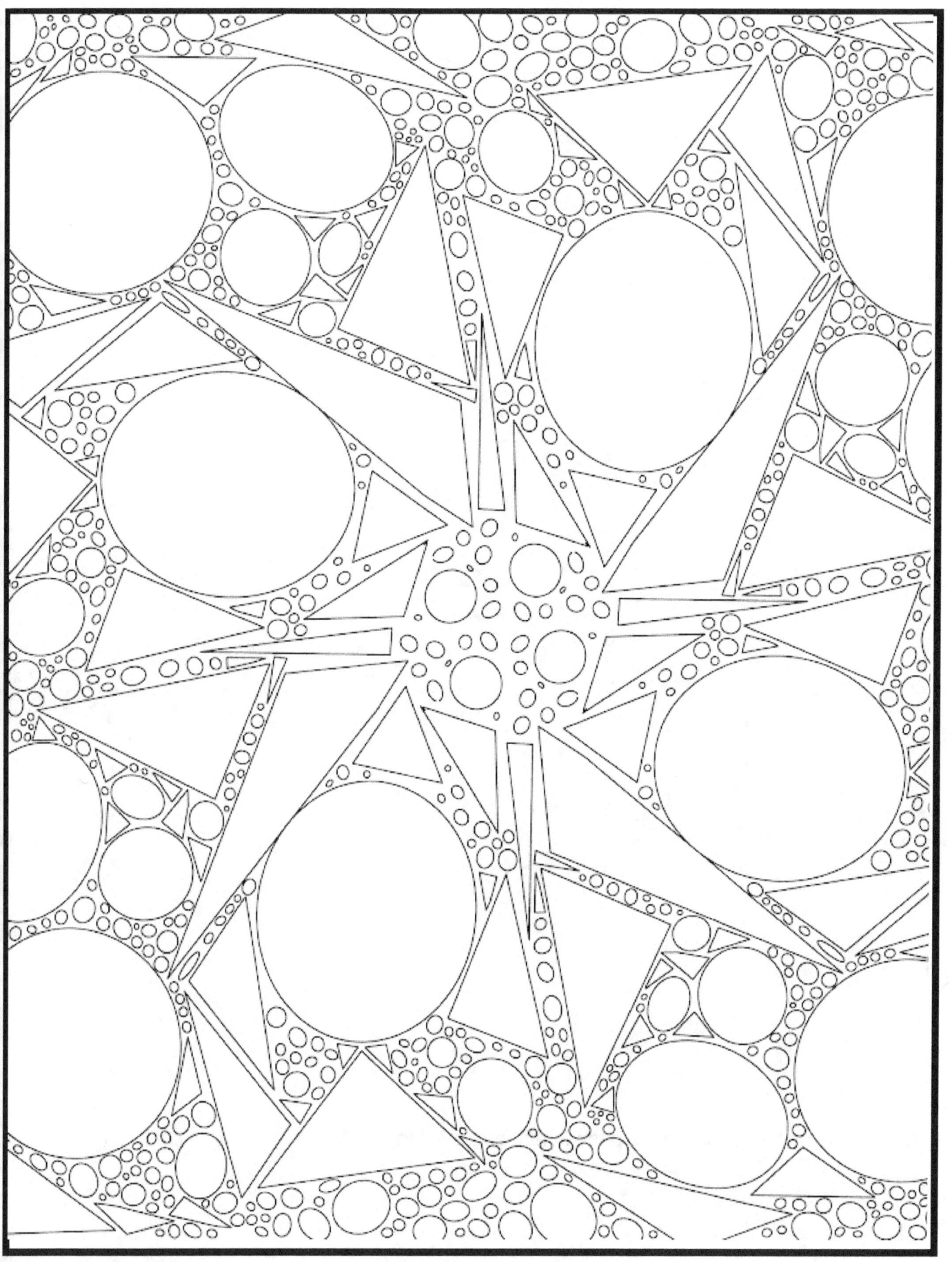

Colouring challenge: divide the page in half and challenge a friend to a speed colouring session

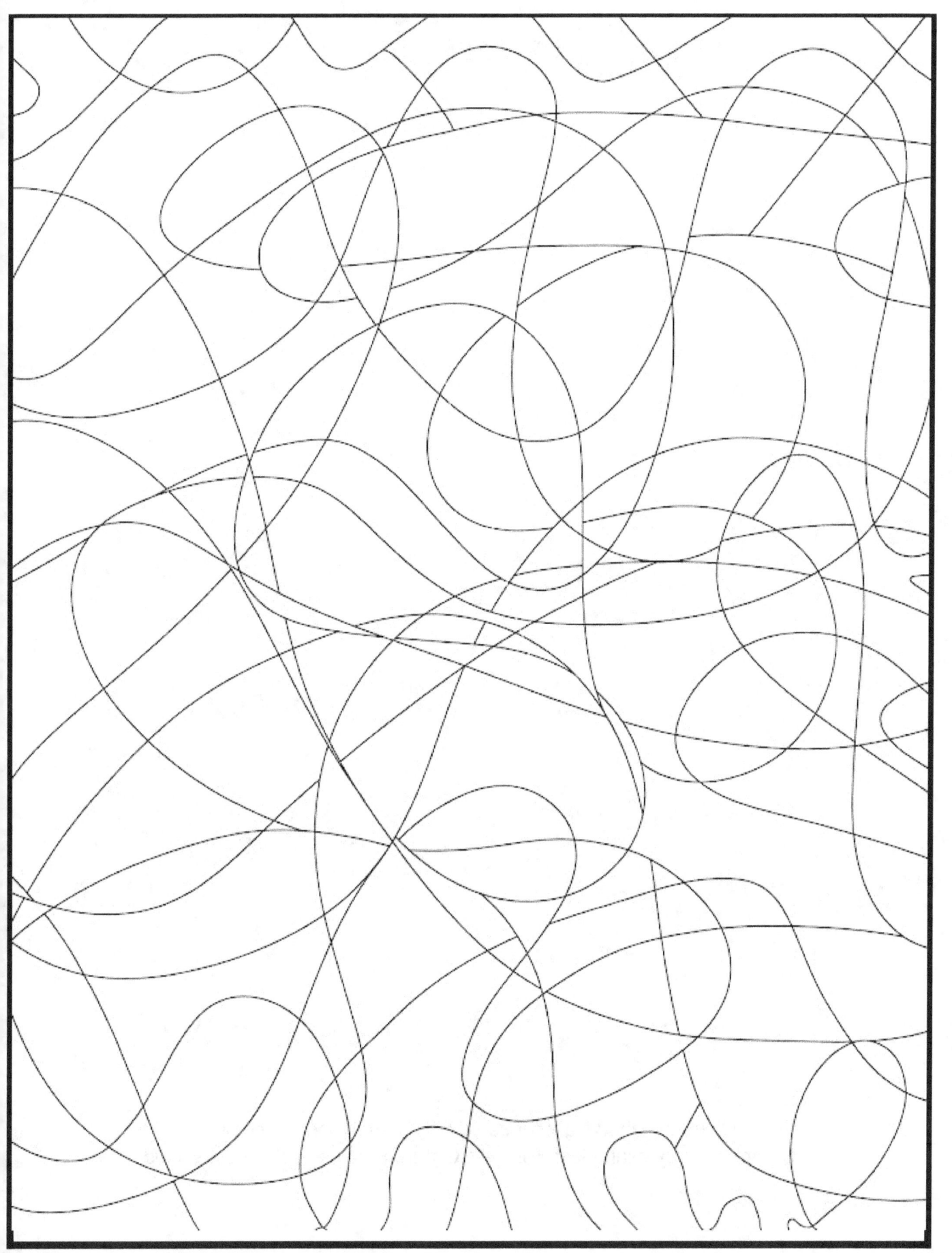

Colouring challenge: try using only complimentary colours
Complimentary examples: Yellow & Green, Blue & Red, Yellow & Red

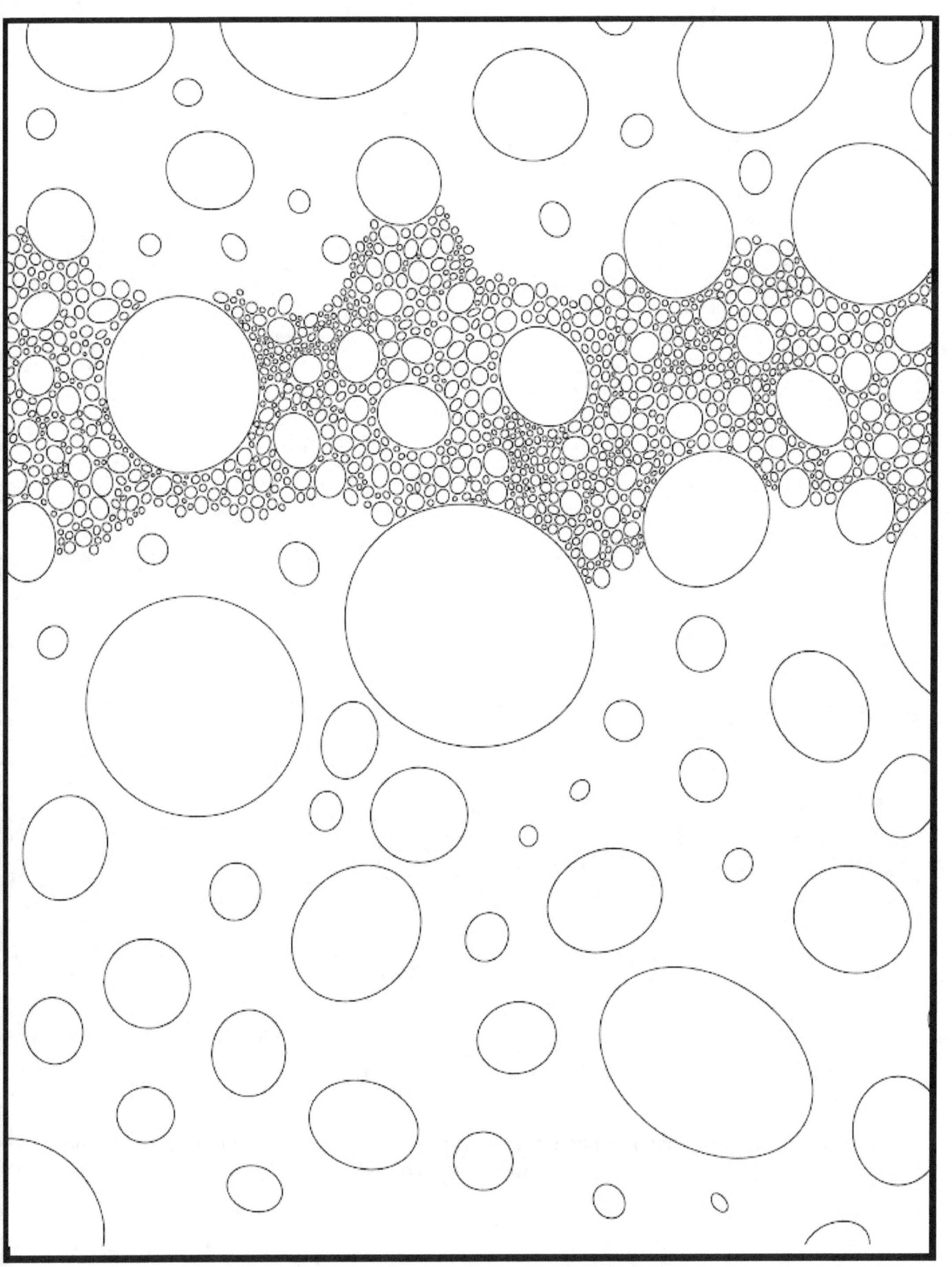

Colouring challenge: choose a corner to start a rainbow pattern and work across to the opposite corner

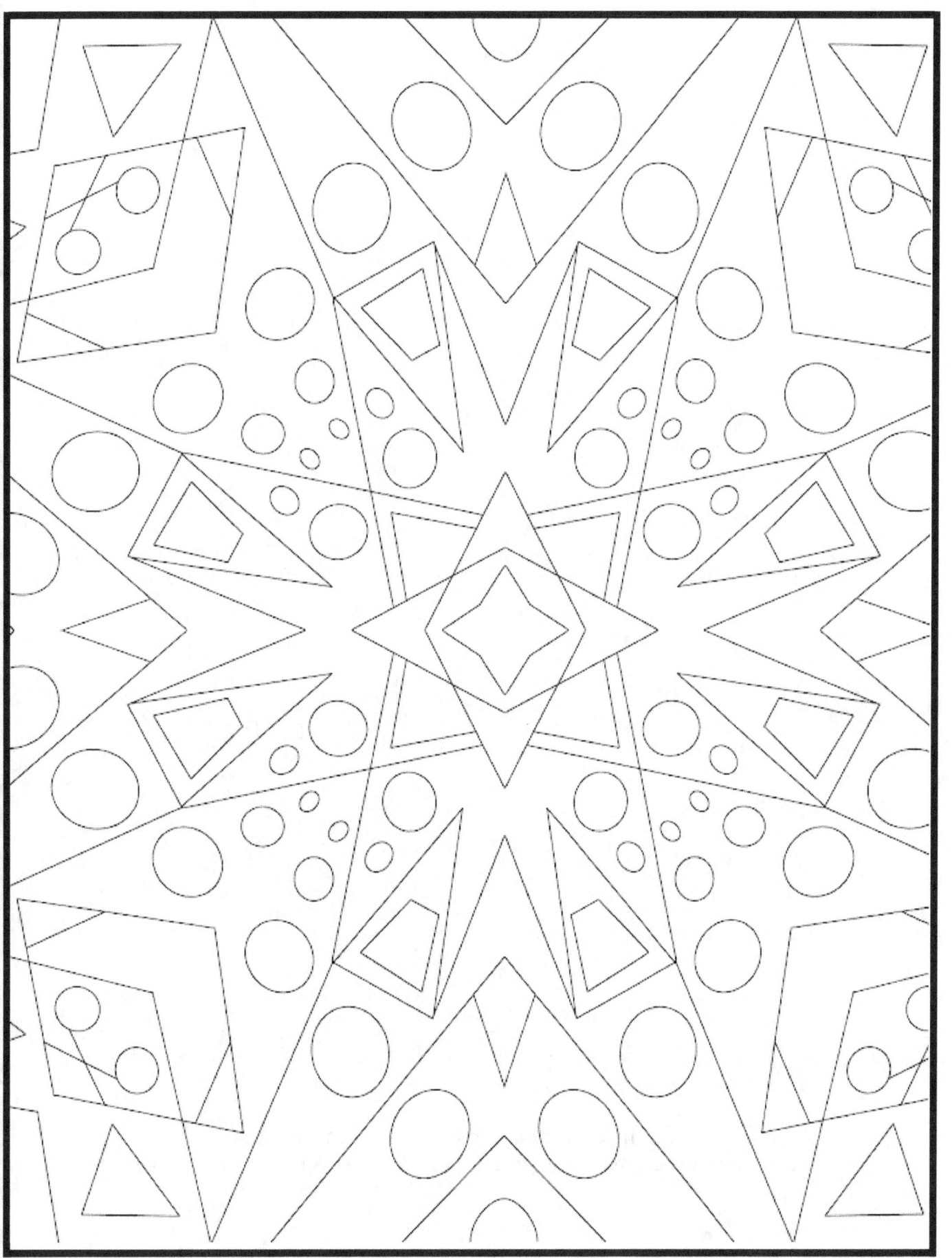

Colouring challenge: use typical seasonal colours
Seasonal examples: Autumn - orange, yellow and brown. Spring - green, yellow, pink

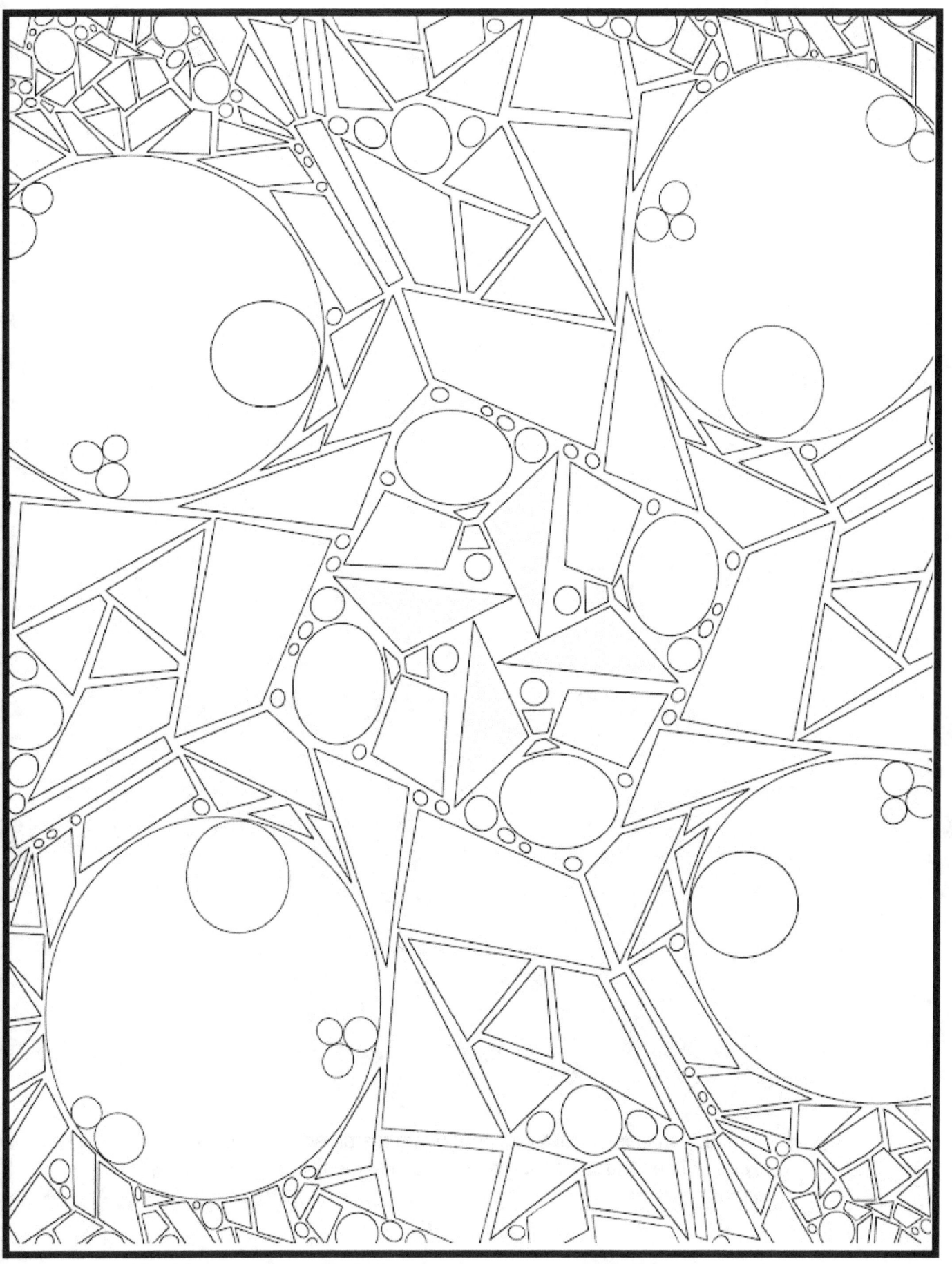

Colouring challenge: turn this image into a stained glass wondow
Darken the lines with a black marker and use mostly primary colours

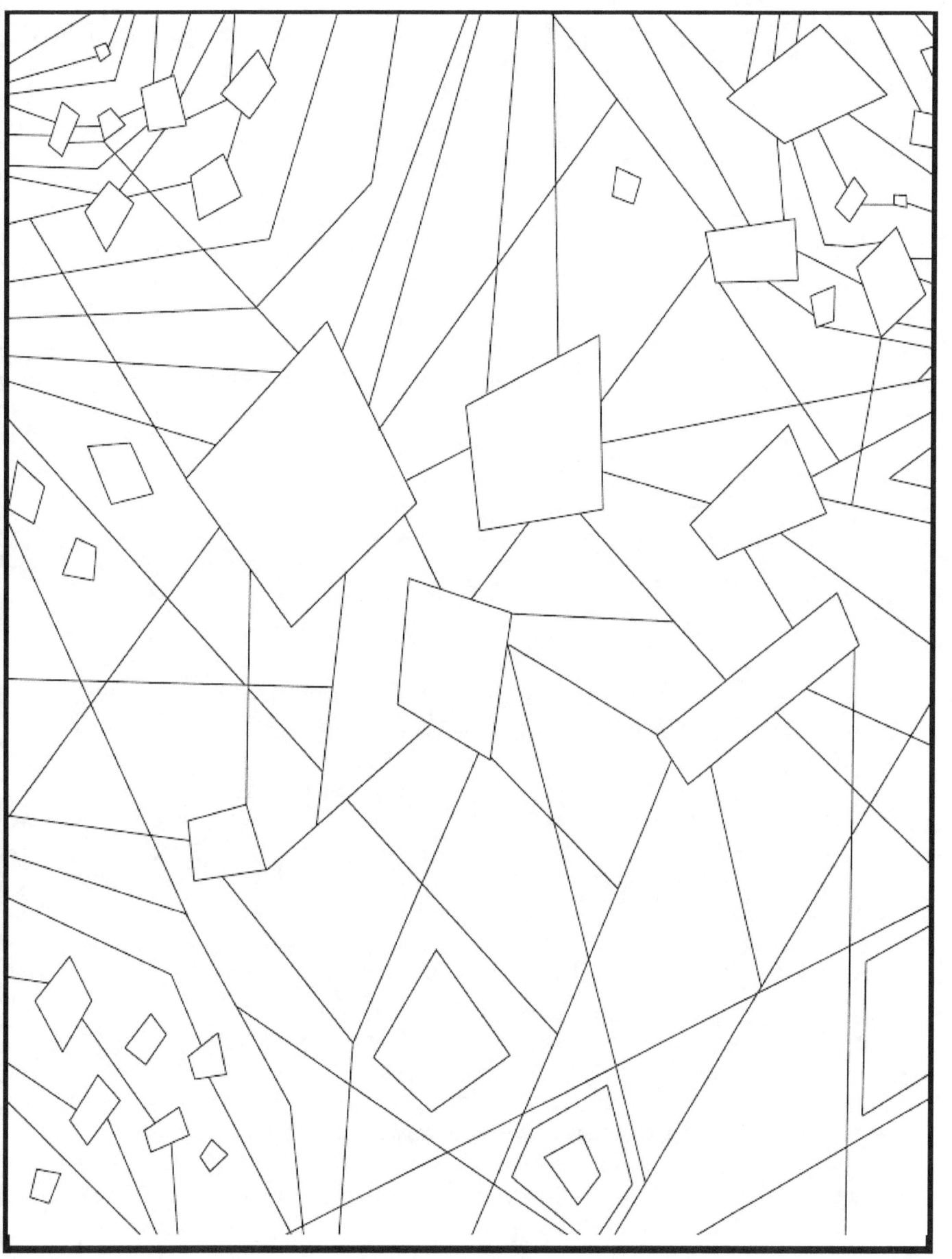

Colouring challenge: use the colours from your country's flag

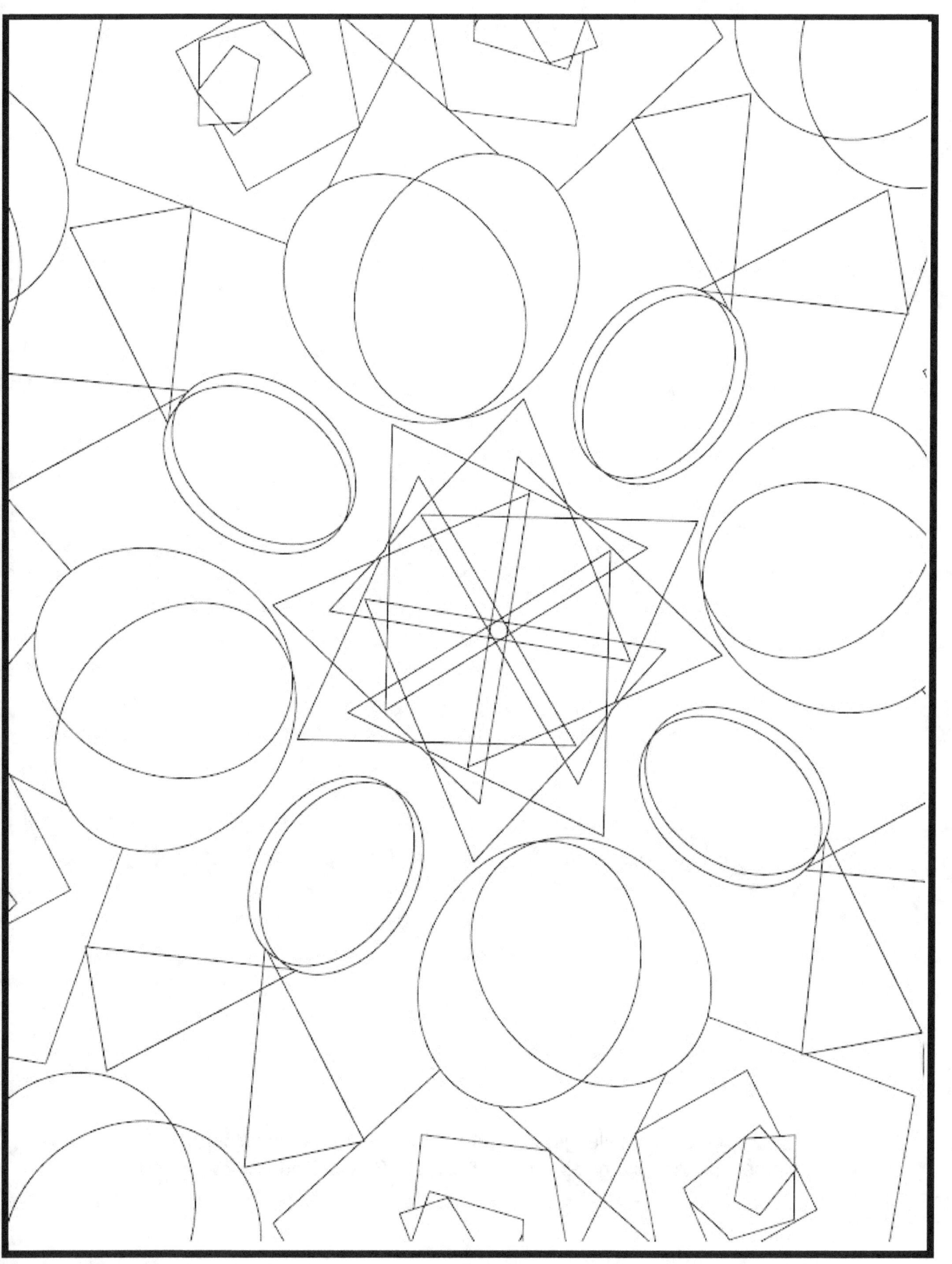

Colouring challenge: try using only complimentary colours
Complimentary examples: Yellow & Green, Blue & Red, Yellow & Red

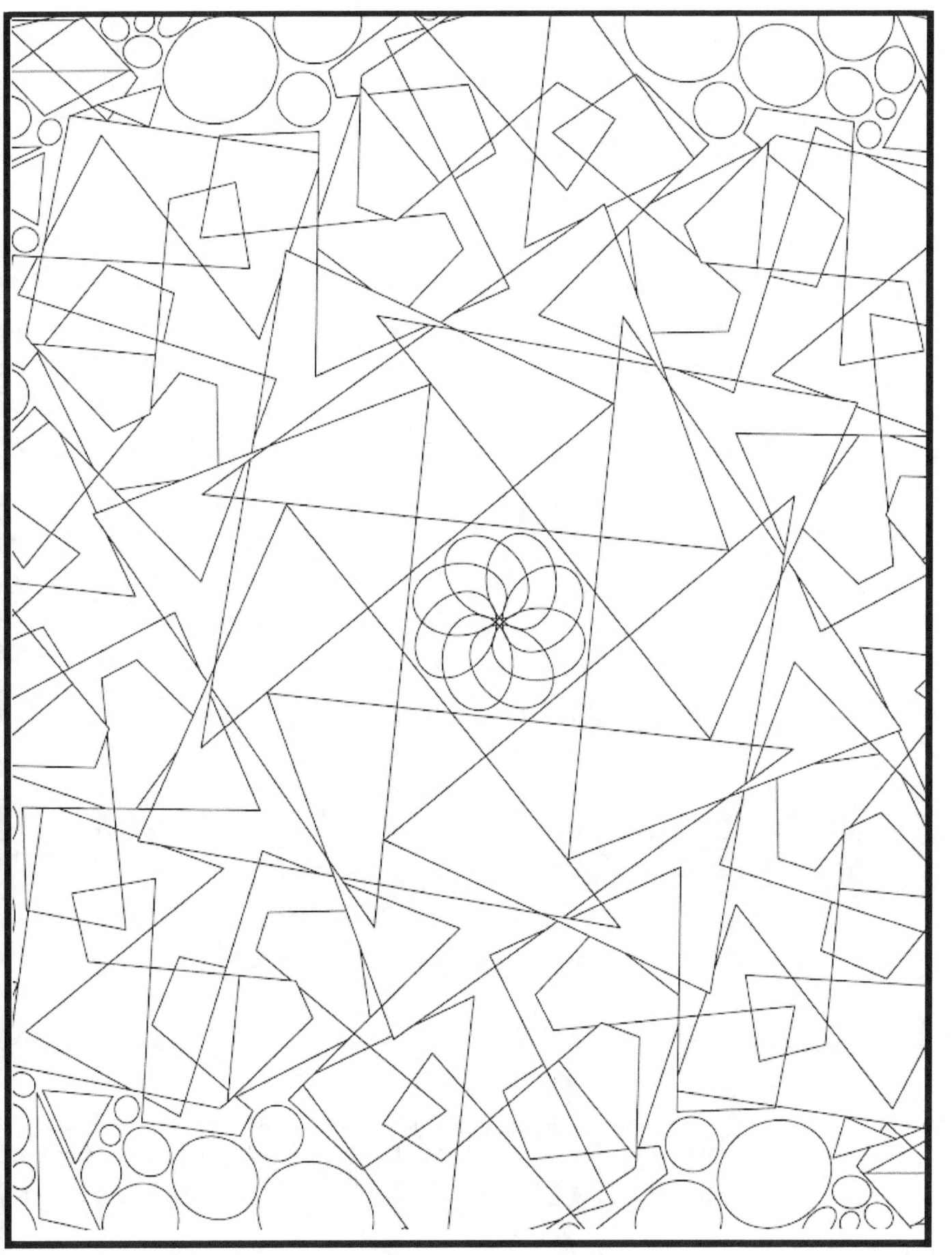

Colouring challenge: try using four random colours
Randomising methods: have a family member choose, blindfold yourself, pour out your supplies and choose those pointing North

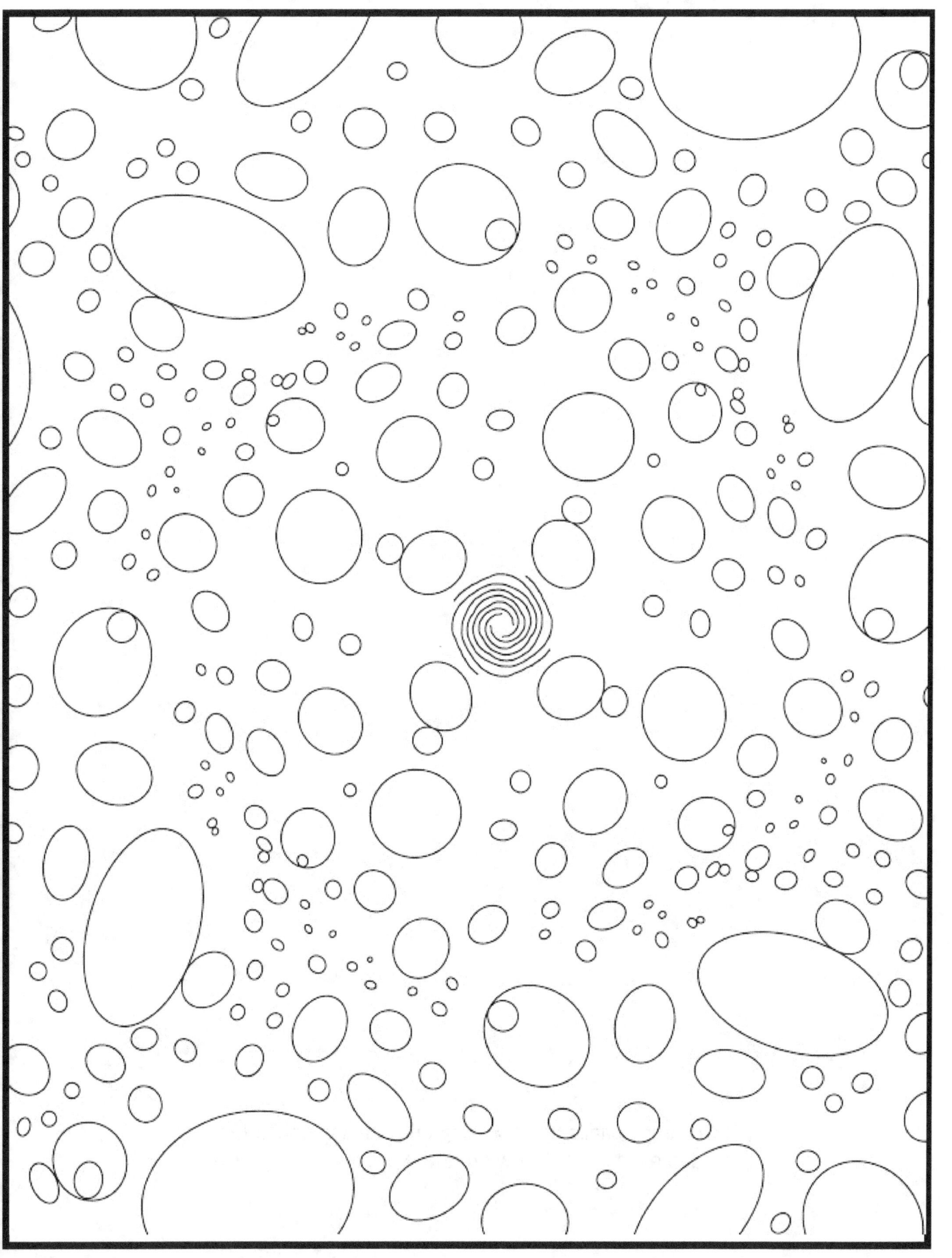

Colouring challenge: try using only hues of one colour
Hue examples: Yellow orange, Yellow, Green yellow

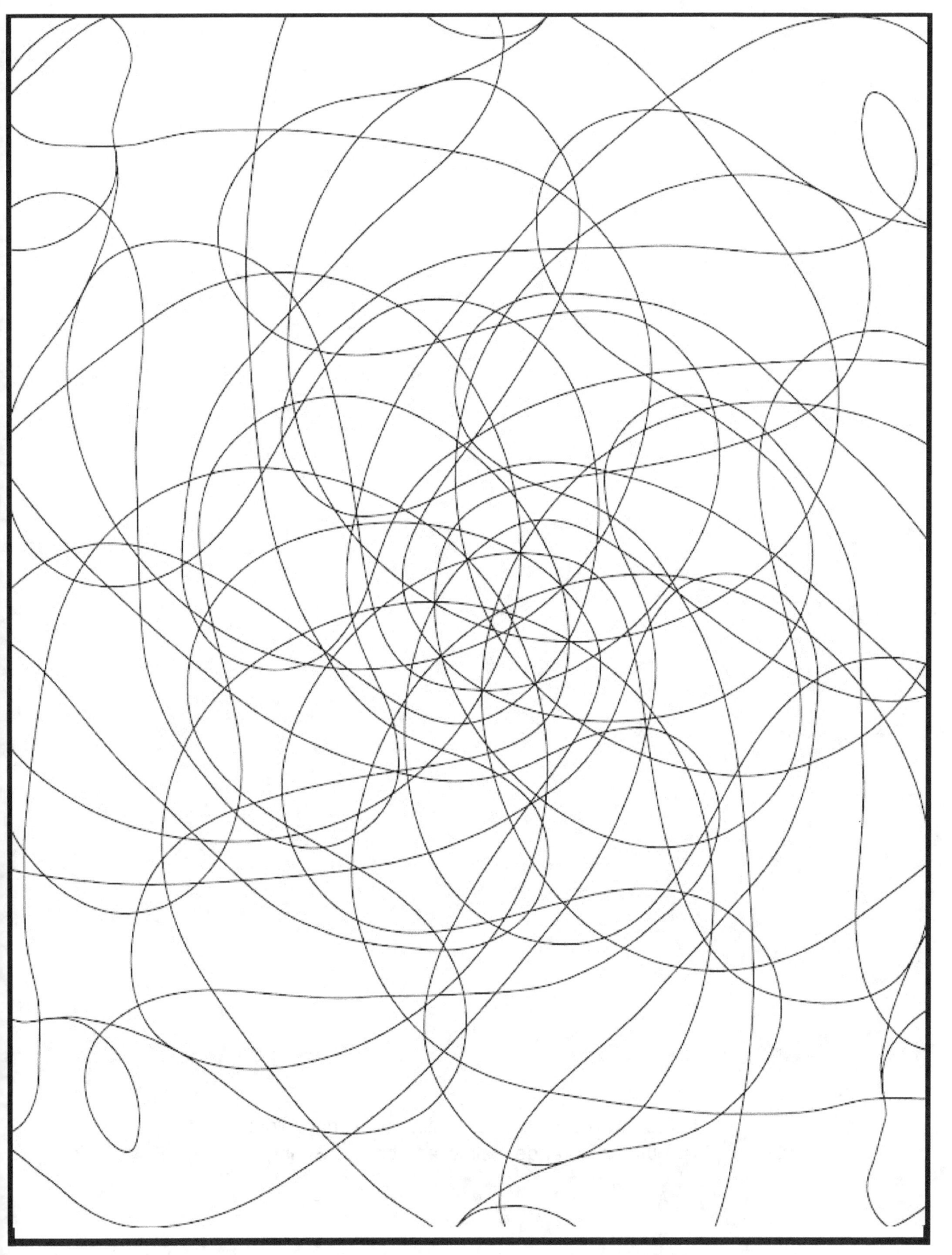

Colouring challenge: use typical seasonal colours
Seasonal examples: Autumn - orange, yellow and brown. Spring - green, yellow, pink

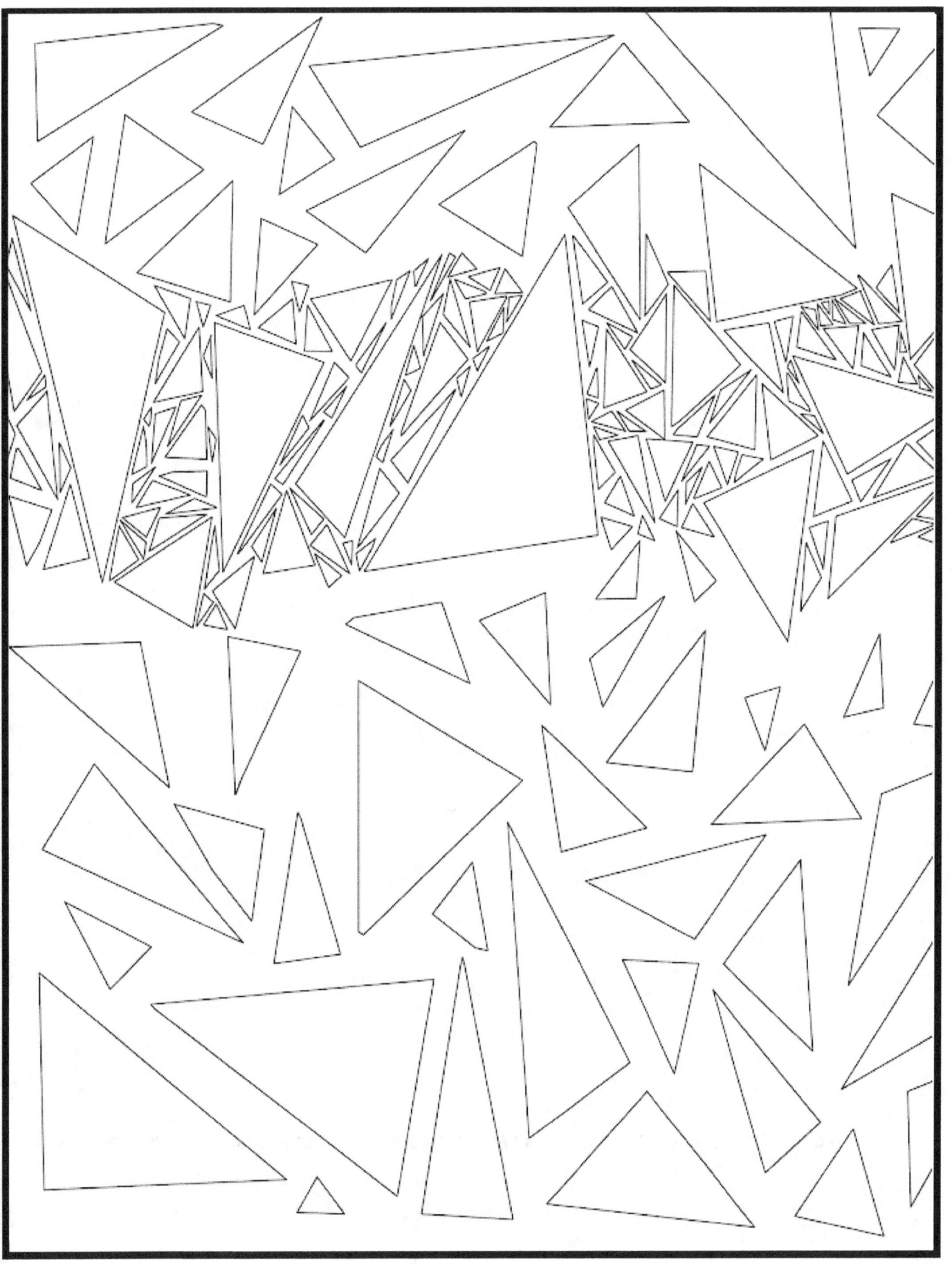

Colouring challenge: divide the page in half and challenge a friend to a speed colouring session

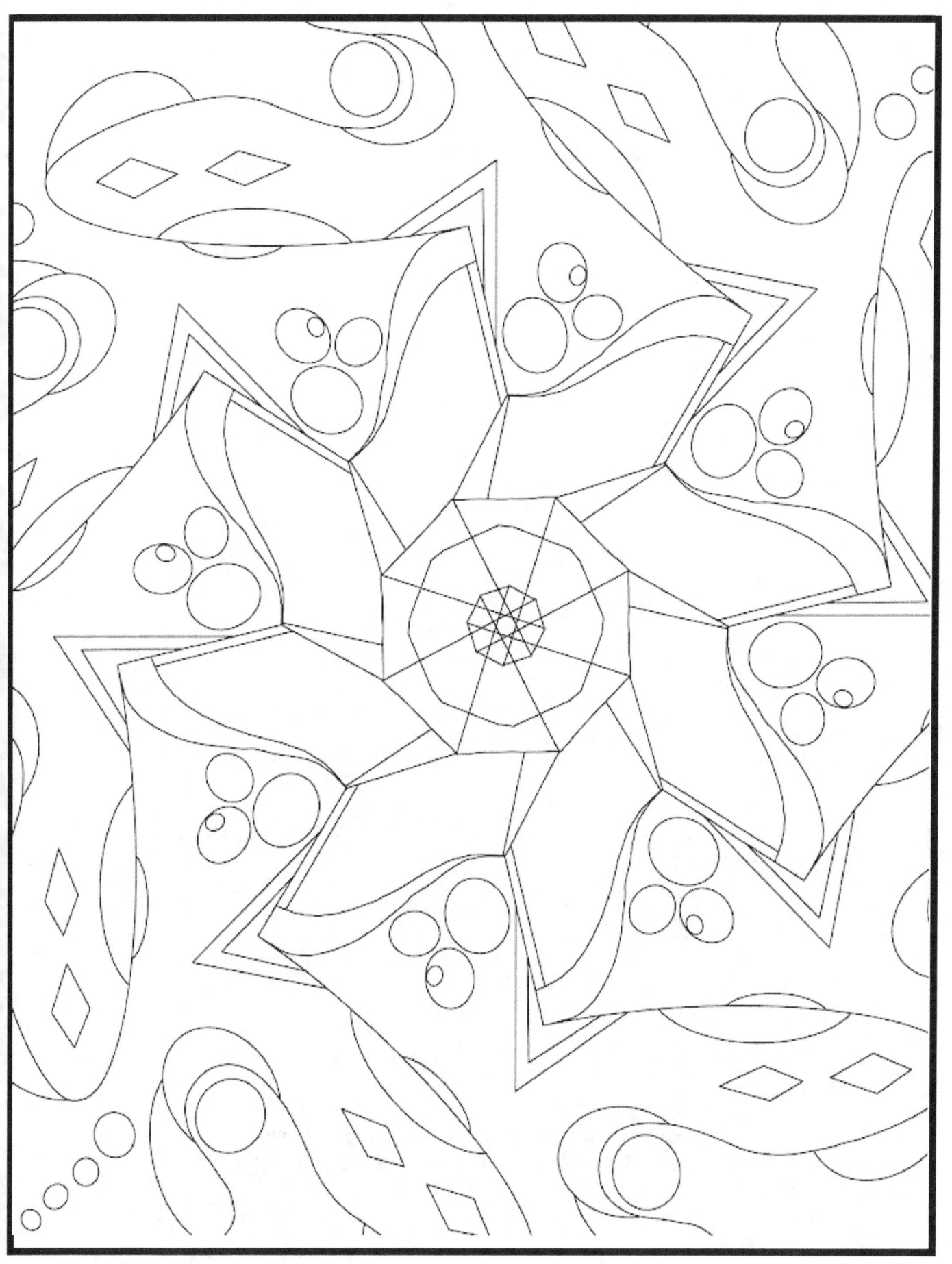

Colouring challenge: colour this in grey scale
Grey scale: leave spaces white, use black and grey

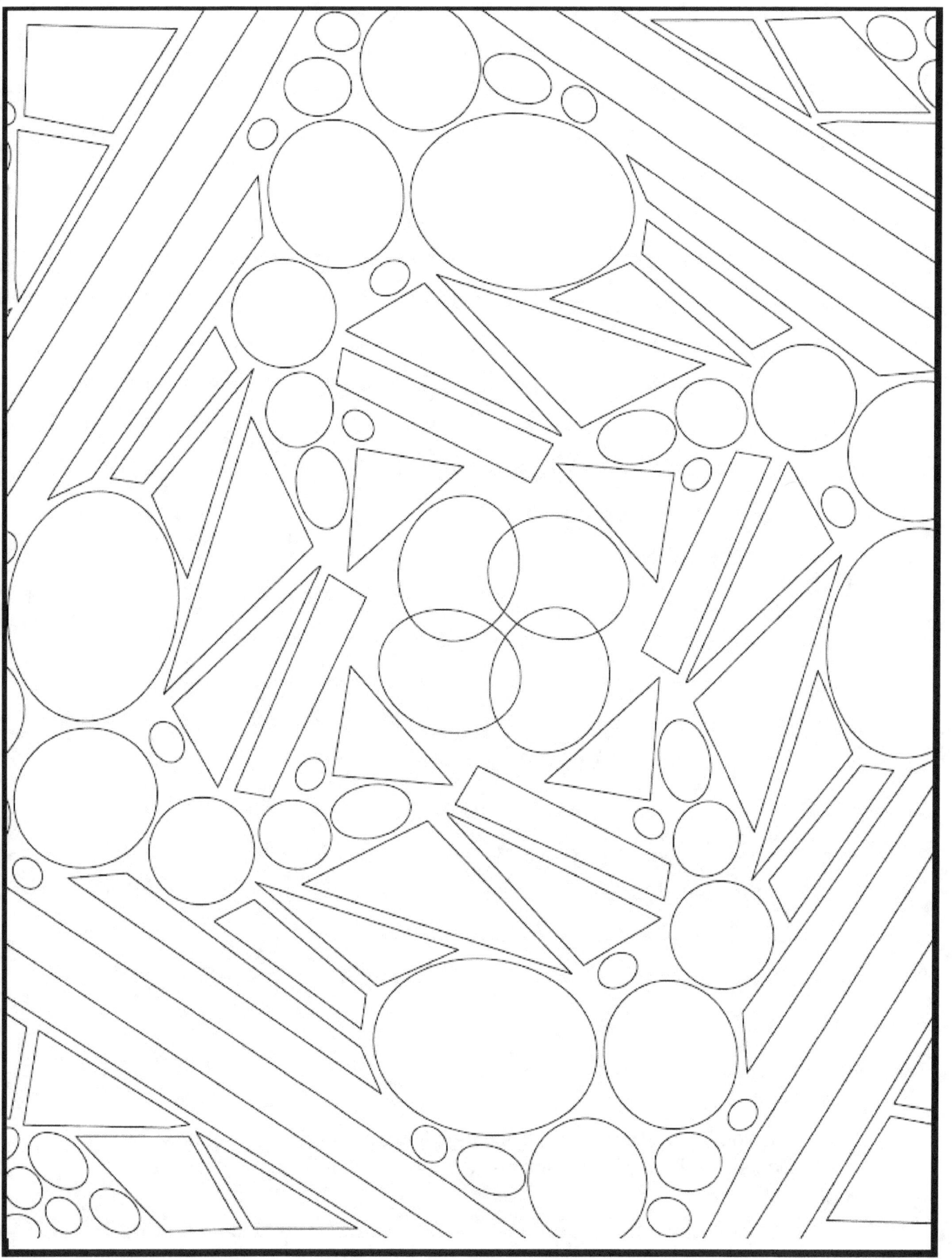

Colouring challenge: turn this image into a stained glass wondow
Darken the lines with a black marker and use mostly primary colours

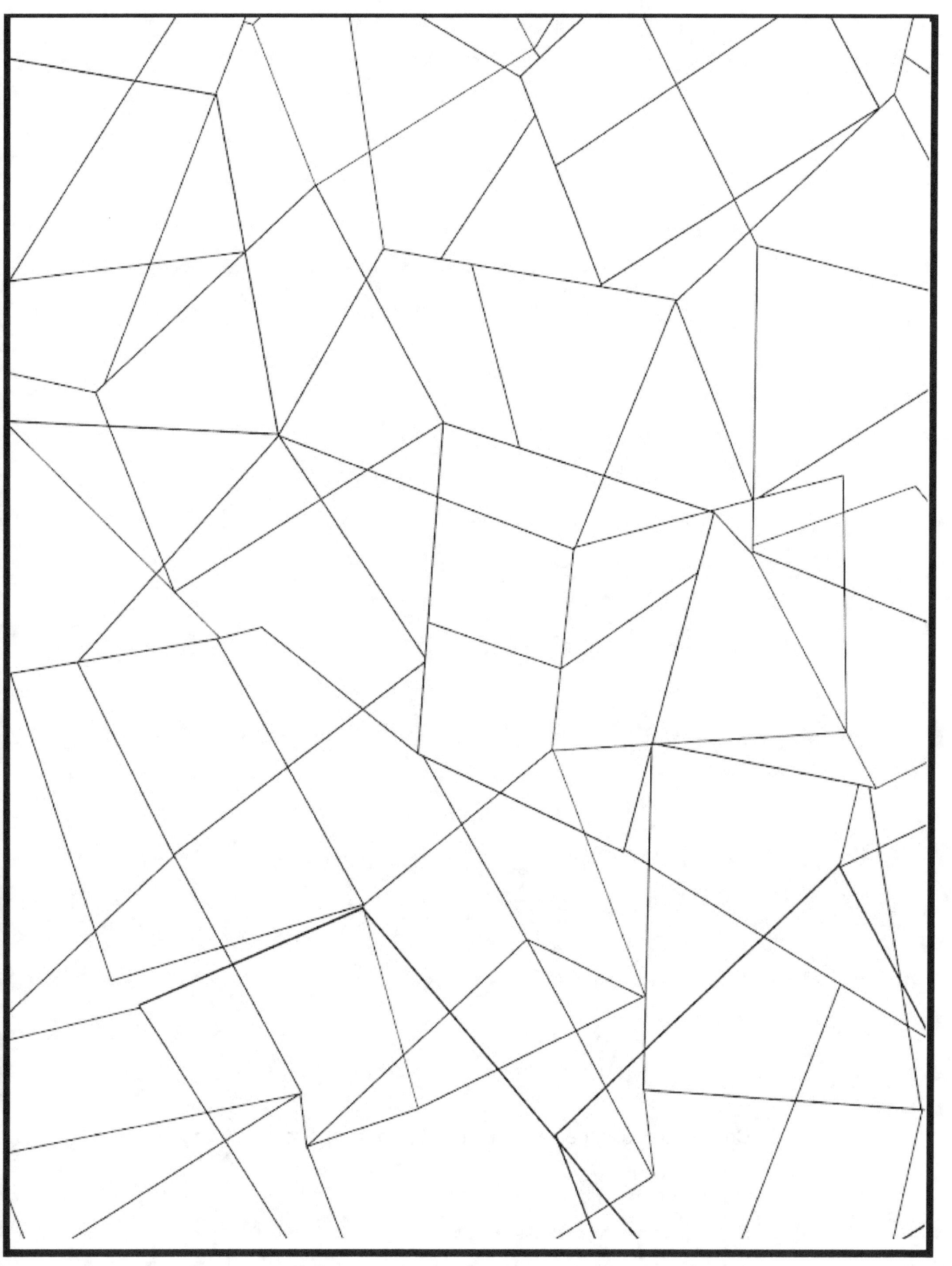

Colouring challenge: use the colours from your country's flag

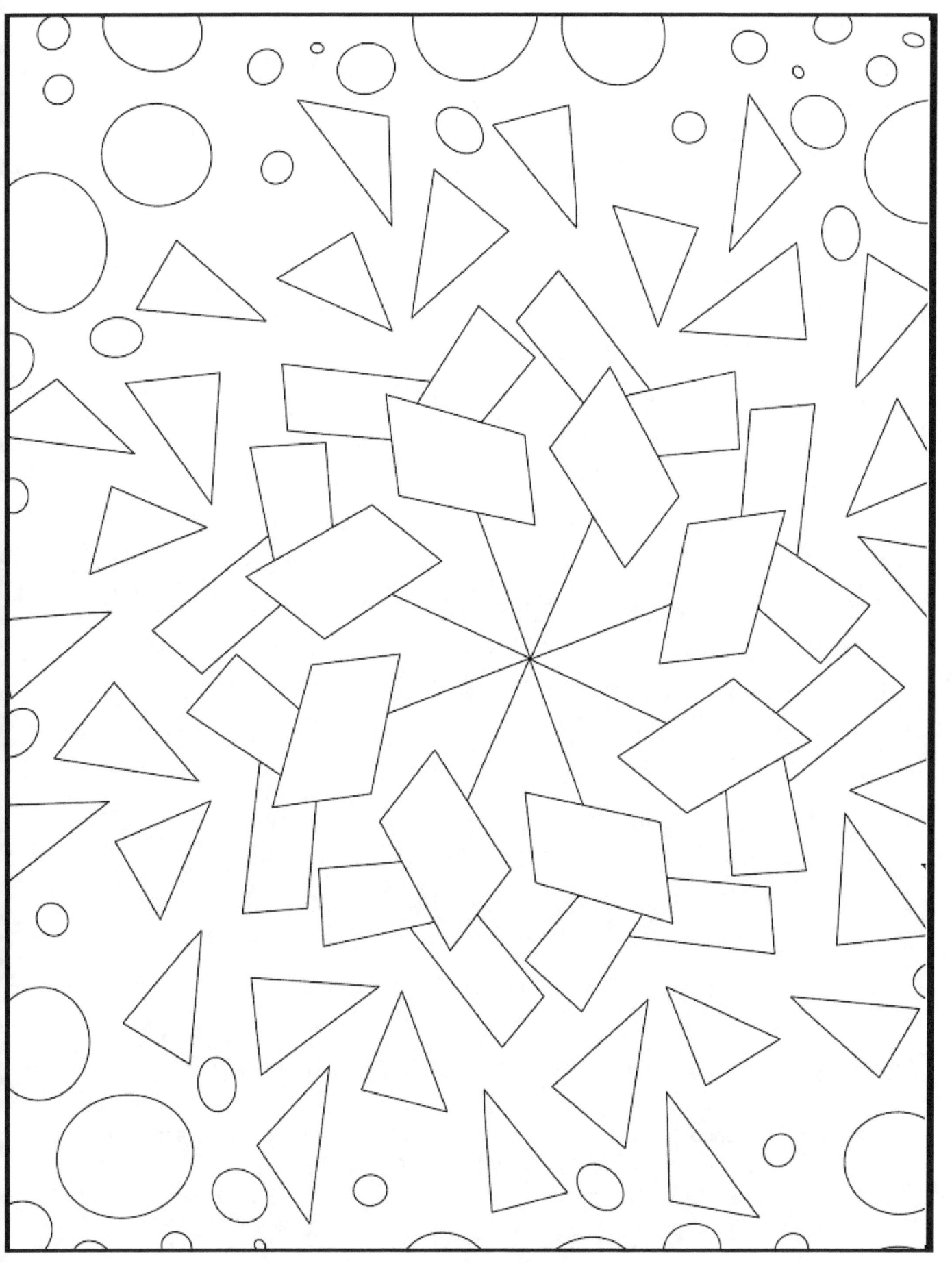

Colouring challenge: choose a corner to start a rainbow pattern and work across to the opposite corner

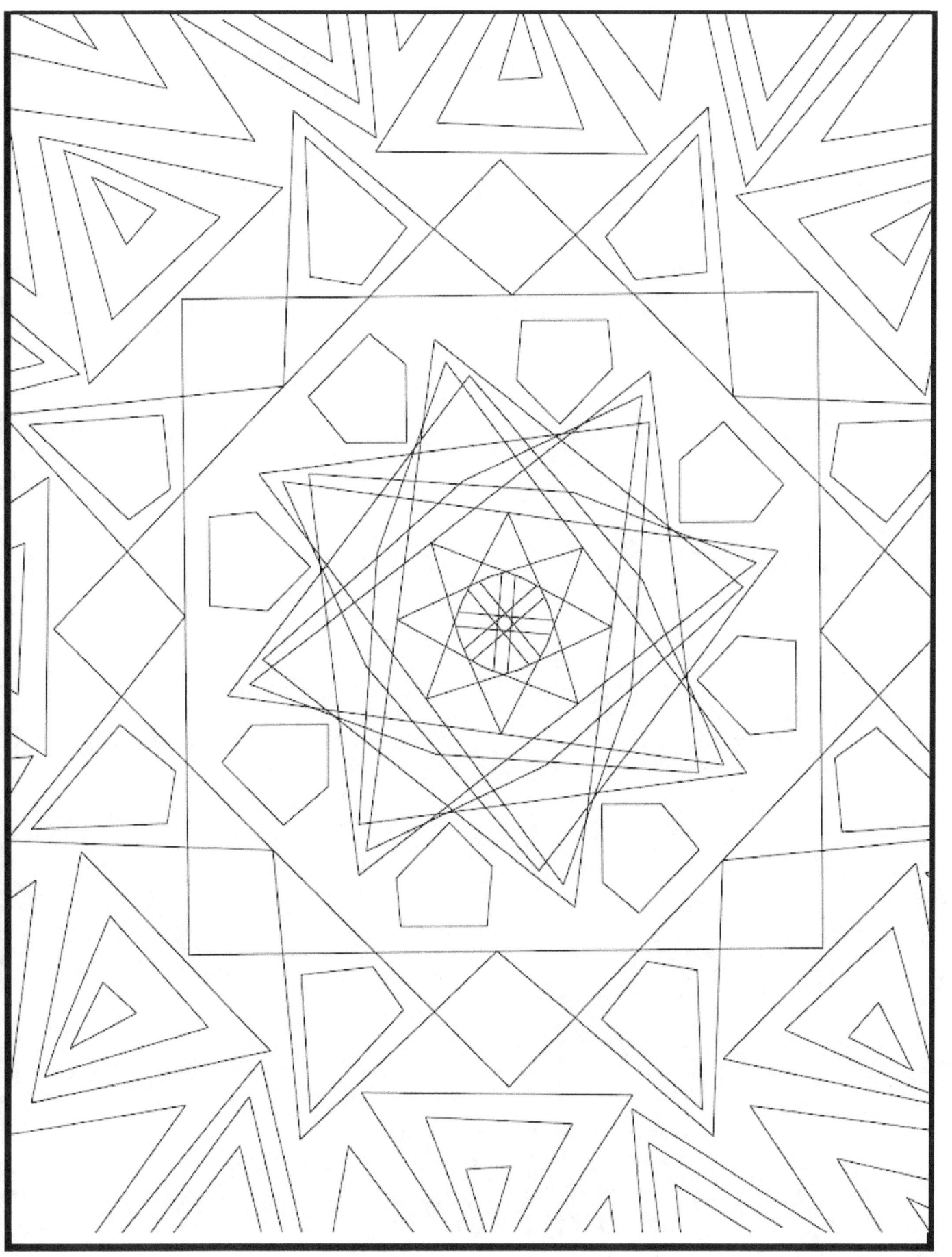

Colouring challenge: use colours related to trees
Typical tree colours: green, brown, orange, yellow

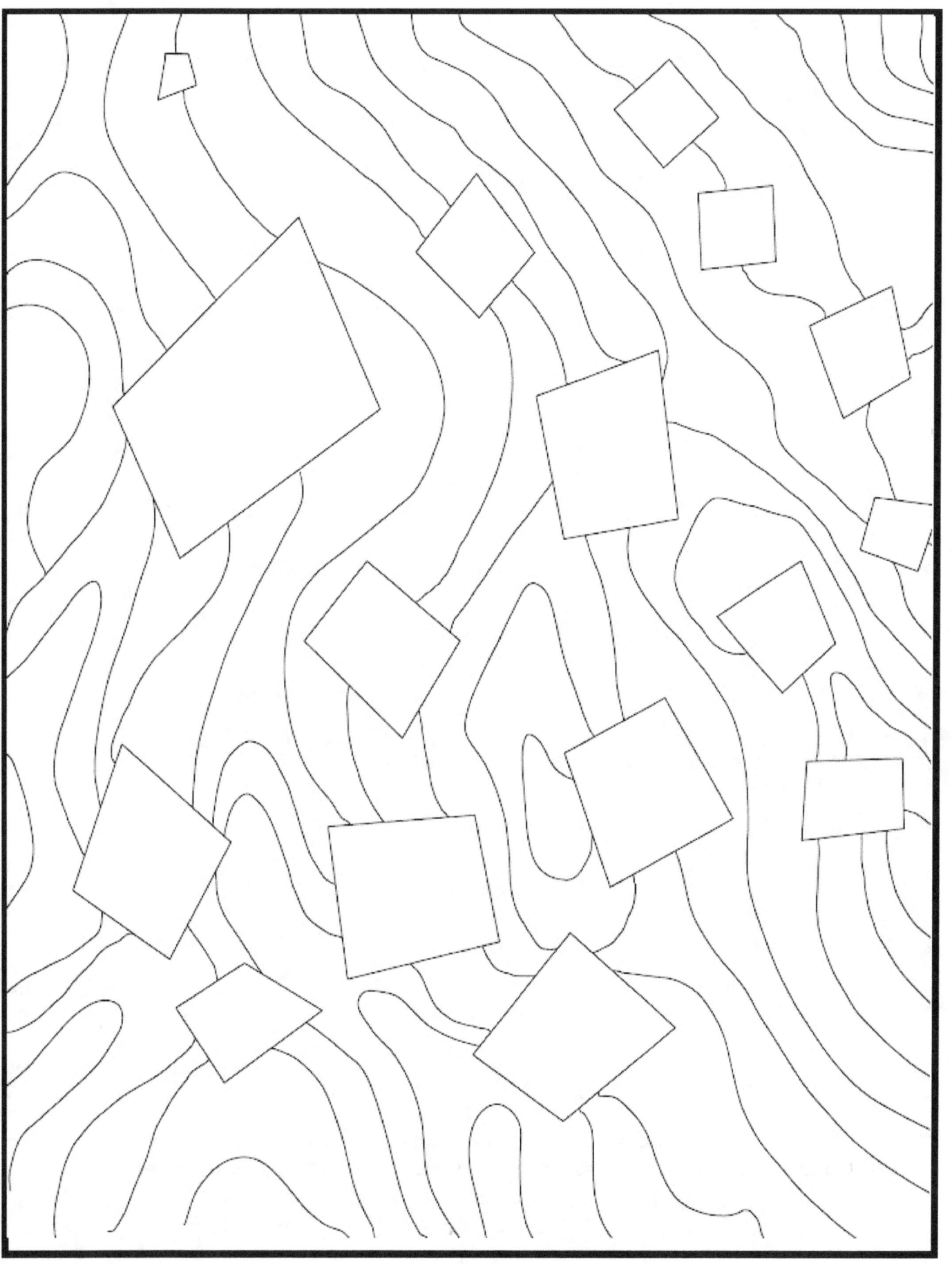

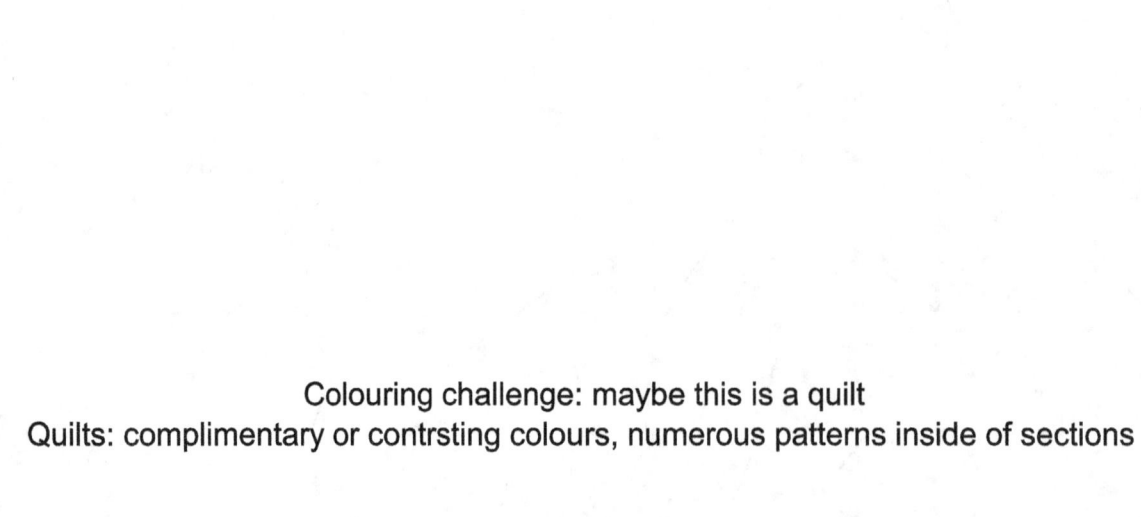

Colouring challenge: maybe this is a quilt
Quilts: complimentary or contrsting colours, numerous patterns inside of sections

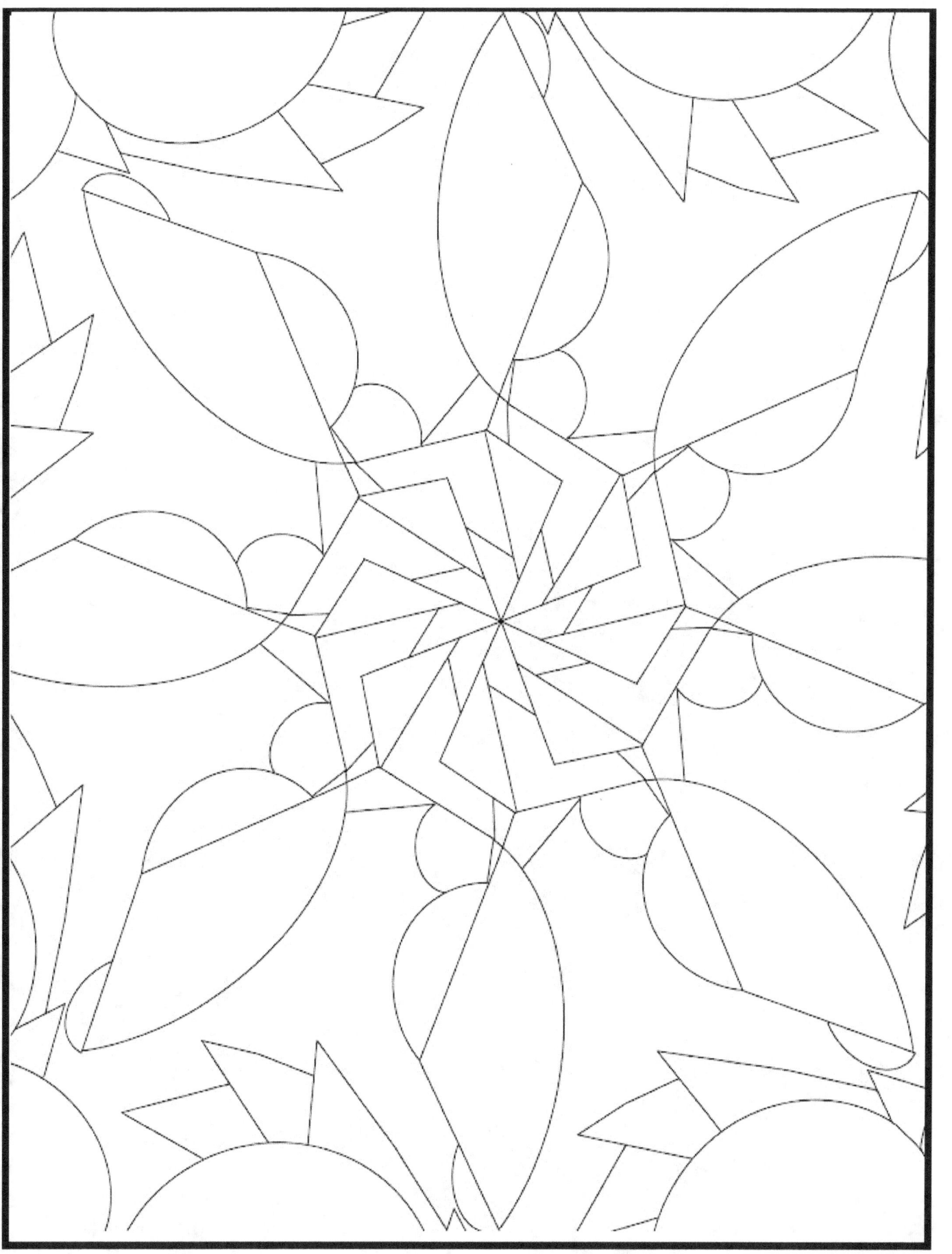

Colouring challenge: use the colours from your country's flag

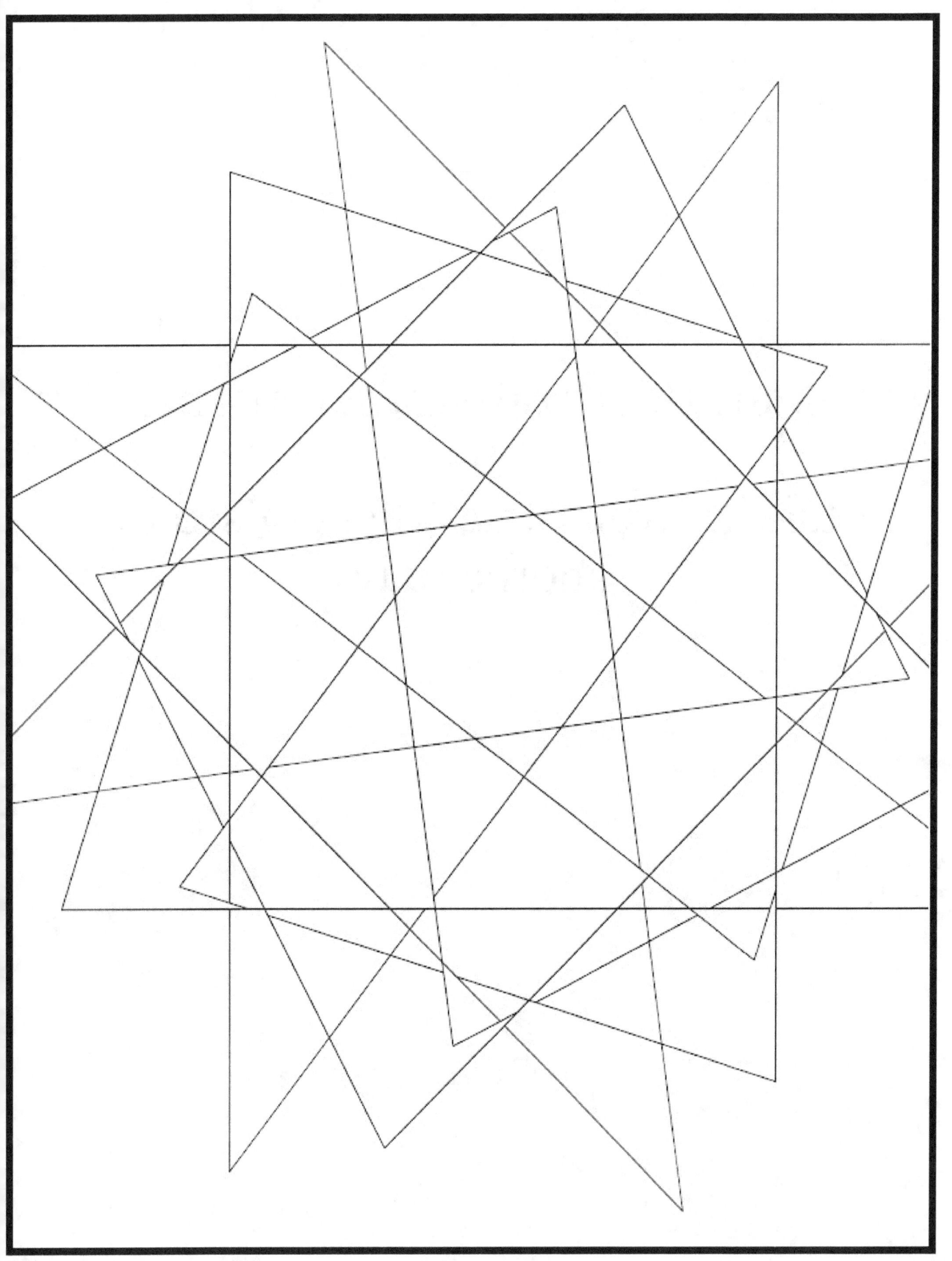

Hopefully these pages gave you a moment to
take a breath and get energised for another day.

www.ingramcontent.com/pod-product-compliance
Lightning Source LLC
Chambersburg PA
CBHW080908220526
45466CB00011BA/3513